MY FIRST LOOK AT WEATHER

LIGHTNING LIGHTS UP THE NIGHT SKY

Lightning

MARIA HIDALGO

CREATIVE EDUCATION

Published by Creative Education

123 South Broad Street, Mankato, Minnesota 56001

Creative Education is an imprint of The Creative Company

Designed by Rita Marshall

Photographs by Getty Image (Adam Jones), JLM Visuals (Doug Reid), Library of Congress,

Tom Stack & Associates (Spencer Swanger, William L. Wantland), Weatherstock

(Warren Faidley)

Copyright © 2007 Creative Education

Printed in the United States of America

Library of Congress Cataloging-in-Publication Data

Hidalgo, Maria. Lightning / by Maria Hidalgo.

p. cm. — (My first look at weather)

Includes index.

ISBN-13 : 978-1-58341-450-7

1. Lightning—Juvenile literature. I. Title. II. Series.

QC966.5.H53 2005   551.56'32—dc22   2005050680

First edition 9 8 7 6 5 4 3 2 1

LIGHTNING

Flashes in the Sky

The sky gets dark as clouds cover the sun. As rain falls, you watch for lightning—bright streaks of light in the sky. Lightning can be scary, but it also can be beautiful.

Lightning happens only during rainstorms. **Electricity** builds up in clouds and on the ground. Lightning is electricity that moves between the clouds and the ground. The flashes of light are called "bolts."

LIGHTNING BOLTS DURING A STORM

Lightning is very hot and powerful. It can start fires and even melt metal. It often hits tall objects. This is why many trees are struck by lightning.

THUNDER

Many kids are frightened by thunder. The big booms during a storm can be so loud that they rattle windows! But thunder cannot hurt people.

LIGHTNING SOMETIMES HITS TALL BUILDINGS

Lightning causes thunder. The electricity heats up the air so much and so fast that it **explodes**. This makes the loud sound that we call thunder.

Light travels faster than sound. That is why you see lightning first and then hear the thunder. For every five seconds you count in between lightning and thunder, the storm is one mile (1.6 km) away!

Lightning travels at a speed
of 224,000 miles (360,000 km)
per hour. That's fast!

LIGHTNING CAN SPLIT INTO MANY BRANCHES

Studying Lightning

Some **scientists** study lightning. A scientist named Benjamin Franklin was one of the first people to think lightning was electricity. He did dangerous **experiments** about 200 years ago to prove his idea.

BENJAMIN FRANKLIN STUDIED LIGHTNING

Franklin flew a kite in a storm using wire instead of string. Lightning hit his kite and sent electricity down the wire. This caused a spark. It proved that Franklin was right!

About 100 years ago, another scientist named Nikola Tesla did experiments. He used electricity to make his own lightning bolts. He used what he learned to make electricity safer for people's homes.

THE ELECTRICITY IN CLOUDS CAUSES LIGHTNING

LIGHTNING SAFETY

Lightning can be very dangerous. But there are ways to keep yourself safe. As soon as you see dark clouds and think a storm is coming, go inside. When there is lightning, stay away from metal things that might carry electricity.

You are safe in a building or a car. If you are not close to buildings when a storm starts, stay away from trees or tall poles. Look for a

Every lightning bolt is actually
made of 10 to 15 flashes.
But they are too fast to see!

SOMETIMES LIGHTNING LOOKS COLORFUL

ditch or another place that lets you get down low. You will be safer in a low place.

If you are in a safe place, it can be fun to watch the bright flashes and count how far away the storm is. Some people call lightning "nature's fireworks." Stay safe and enjoy the show!

LIGHTNING CAN BE EXCITING TO WATCH

Hands-on: Fingertip Lightning

Try this activity to make mini lightning bolts.

What You Need

A plastic comb
A piece of dry wool, like a wool sweater
A door with a metal doorknob in a dark room

What You Do

1. Rub the comb back and forth on the wool. This builds up electricity.
2. Slowly bring the comb near the metal doorknob.

You should see a tiny spark jump between the comb and the doorknob. This is what happens between a storm cloud and the ground. Electricity is moving from one place to another!

ELECTRICITY CAN MAKE HAIR STAND UP

Index

Words to Know

electricity—a kind of energy that turns on lights and makes machines run

experiments—tests that are done to find out if something is true or not

explodes—gets much bigger or spreads out very quickly

scientists—people who study nature, space, or other parts of science

Read More

Branley, Franklyn M. *Flash, Crash, Rumble, and Roll*. New York: HarperCollins Children's Books, 1999.

Mack, Lorrie. *Eye Wonder: Weather*. New York: Dorling Kindersley Limited, 2004.

Sherman, Josepha. *Nature's Fireworks: A Book About Lightning*. Minneapolis: Picture Window Books, 2003.

Explore the Web

The Storm http://www.wcmsolutions.com/products/thestorm/index.html

Lightning Photos http://www.fema.gov/kids/thphot.htm

Kidstorm: Lightning http://skydiary.com/kids/lightning.html